C000176586

When We
Were Young

THE *1950s*

When We Were Young

THE 1950s

Tony Husband

ARCTURUS

ARCTURUS

This edition published in 2017 by Arcturus Publishing Limited
26/27 Bickels Yard, 151–153 Bermondsey Street,
London SE1 3HA

ISBN: 978-1-78428-694-1
AD005574UK

Printed in Italy

Contents

Business as usual

The 1950s were a decade of conformity: men went out to work, while women stayed at home to look after the children. The British were still recovering from war and welcomed the return of boring, everyday life after so much sacrifice. Rationing lasted until 1954, but people were slowly acquiring consumer goods. Most homes had a vacuum cleaner, cooker and fridge. Soon they'd have televisions...

'Maybe we have lost the Empire, Vera, but I'm happy
to swap it for a nice home in the suburbs, a little car
and all mod cons.'

'Darling, we've become boring and I like it.'

'It's grand to be back at work after all that
regimentation in the army.'

The decade began with biblical amounts of rain.
'And the referee is out now inspecting the pitch.'

Rationing persisted.
'No more, Mum?! But the war finished years ago.'

Wildlife was abundant back then, and so were lollipop men and women.

People dressed up, not down. 'Yes, dear, you look very smart, but you're only going to dig the allotment.'

'Apparently, Britain leads the world in science, industry,
commerce and the arts, so how come we can only afford
jam sandwiches for dinner?'

17

*Shops shut on the dot at 6.00pm. 'You've exactly
45 seconds to finish your shopping, love.'*

But things were looking up. Factories built to supply
weapons were adapted to help make homes.

'I don't care how much they flippin' cost! Go down the
shop and buy one now, Phillip.'

21

Car ownership spread. 'Darling, I wish you paid as much attention to me as you do to that car.'

Caravans became popular,
but not if you ended up behind one.

It was a very different world.
'Oh, let her have one. What harm can it do?'

'I think it's ludicrous only having 12 pubs in the village'

'Look: three bedrooms, medium–size garden, small drive, and they're asking for £3,000... extortionate!!'

It was the golden age of DIY.

'What did we do to deserve free medical care in the
NHS? Ooh, let me think. Well, we did win the war.'

'Well, after the long years of fighting, it's great to have peace again.'

*There was a hero in every pub. 'So I'm surrounded by
enemy patrols, I've got my tommy gun in my hand and...'*

'He's 12 and, with things being so tight, this is the first
birthday cake we've been able to make for him.'

'And another thing: I was forced to eat frog spawn in milk at school lunch.'

'I can't decide whether our baby looks more like
Nikita Khrushchev or Winston Churchill.'

'Now, children, remember... the government says if we're attacked with nuclear weapons, hide under the bed and put your hands over your ears.'

'No, dear, I don't think the Suez Crisis will reach us here
on the Shropshire canal.'

'Wines? Yes, we've this one or that one – red or white.'

'Make us a cuppa, will you, lovey?'

The good times are back

Living standards were on the rise, but things were very different from today. People took holidays in British seaside resorts. Houses were heated with coal or by electric fires. The rag and bone man was a regular sight, and when you returned lemonade bottles to the shop you'd receive 3d deposit. And lots of ex-soldiers became PE teachers, which meant kids were in for a tough time.

'There's a shilling for the Saturday matinee, an ice cream
and some chips on the way home.
Bring me back the change.'

'You climb Mount Everest?! Huh, it takes you all your
energy to climb the wooden hill to Bedfordshire.'

Authority was obeyed. 'That policeman says it's getting late – better do as he says and head home.'

'Look at them, thinking they're a cut above, just because
they're going to Southport and not Blackpool.'

'Oh, I hate rush hour. You can't move for all the traffic.'

'I have a vision for the railways. You're not in a rush to get home, are you?'

'We had that new sliced bread last night.
It's the best thing since I don't know what.'

'Your car is black? Erm, nearly all cars are black.'

'I've just caught our daughter watching that... that...
Elvis Presley fellow!!'

'He's done his hip in trying to dribble like
Stanley Matthews.'

'We seem to have been in this pea-souper all day.
We can't be far from London now.'

'Parents are warned to check their children for symptoms
of what is known as "a teenager".'

'The last dinner lady might have let you off eating greens, but I'm not the last dinner lady.'

'Tell you what, you're not going to get many people going on holidays in one of those. It looks far too dicey.'

'You can't beat Blackpool in the summer.'

'You're not in the Paras any more, Mr Hill. Could you please, erm, demilitarize the PE area?'

The Coronation, 1953: 'And the Queen is looking resplendent in her golden coach drawn by six white steeds... her diamonds glisten in the sun like her smile...'

'Aren't you worried all these modern devices will make
women redundant?'

'You've been to the pub, haven't you?
I've found sawdust in your shoes.'

'Well, I'm the milk monitor: if I want two, I'll have two.'

'Come to Britain for a better life, they said.
No one mentioned the weather.'

'The perfect marriage? I was looking for my own Diana Dors, but I ended up with a Peggy Mount.'

'Your skiffle group may be the next big thing, but I need my washboard back.'

Back then zoos didn't pretend to be anything but entertainment.

Football was different too.
'This is where I always stand.'

The age of plenty

The British weren't exactly rich in the 1950s compared with today, but by the end of the decade they began to feel a lot wealthier. Class divisions were still rigid, smog was terrible and there wasn't much to do, but there was light at the end of the tunnel. As the cult of Elvis Presley crossed the Atlantic, new sub-cultures such as Teddy Boys and Beatniks began to appear, the first sign of the revolution to come.

'There you go, kids: lemonade and crisps.
Mummy and Daddy will be in there for a couple of hours.'

'Standing room only, Mrs Beech. You'll get a seat when
Mr and Mrs Muldoon get off at the Co-op.'

'Tut, tut, I can see you, George.'

'No, I certainly won't teach you to play with your feet
like Jerry Lee Lewis, whoever he may be!'

'I'm worried about my husband, Doctor.
He's started listening to the Goon Show.'

'Shall we go to the Fridge Bar; it's full of cool cats.'

'Rock around the clock?!! You couldn't even rock
around your wrist-watch!'

'Run... Teddy Boys!!' 'What are Teddy Boys?'

'We're thinking of going abroad on holiday.'
'What, to Wales or Scotland?'

NEWS

England 3
Magical
Magyars 6

Hungary humbled England at Wembley in 1953.
'Strange, my daddy says no one beats England.'

There was no such thing as Health & Safety.

'Are those long shorts or short longs?'

'Sit down, dear. Your father is going to warn you about
rock and roll.'

'That's to scare the birds away.
Now I just need something to frighten the kids
from the estate.'

'I'm not sure I can go that fast in my car.'

'John, Paul, stop playing those flipping guitars and take
the blooming bins out.'

'Water tank? No, it's my husband's Brylcreem supply.'

'It's a new programme called The Archers.
Can't see it lasting.'

'I sometimes wish we weren't the first people in the street to have a television.'

'Yes, George, but why a Mini?
How are we both going to fit into that?'

'Stereo!! Two speakers!!
Are you trying to make us both deaf?!'

Donald Campbell kept breaking world speed records.
'We only came out here for a bit of peace and quiet.'

'Sun tan? Yes, we're just back from this little unspoilt
village called Benidorm.'

'So this is the very first British motorway.
But where's the zebra crossing?'